Table of Contents

Chapter 1: Introduction to Solana 1
   Overview of Blockchain Technology 1
   The Emergence of Solana 2

Chapter 2: Understanding the SOL Blockchain 5
   Key Features of Solana 5
   Use Cases for Solana 6

Chapter 3: Solana's Consensus Mechanism: Exploring Proof of History 9
   What is Proof of History? 9
   How Proof of History Works 10
   Benefits of Proof of History 12

Chapter 4: Developing on Solana: Tools and Resources for Developers 14
   Programming Languages Supported 14
   Development Frameworks and Libraries 15
   Resources for Learning and Support 17

Chapter 5: Solana vs. Ethereum: A Comparative Analysis 20
   Performance Metrics 20
   Ecosystem and Community 21
   Use Cases and Adoption 23

Chapter 6: Decentralized Finance (DeFi) on Solana: Trends and Innovations 25
   Overview of DeFi on Solana 25
   Major DeFi Projects 26
   Future of DeFi on Solana 28

Chapter 7: NFT Marketplaces on Solana: Opportunities and Challenges 30
   Overview of NFTs on Solana 30
   Key NFT Marketplaces 31
   Challenges Facing NFT Adoption 33

Chapter 8: Scalability Solutions in Solana: What Sets It Apart 35
   Architecture of Solana 35

Innovations in Scalability 36
  Comparison with Other Blockchains...38

Chapter 9: Security Features of the Solana Blockchain............41
  Security Protocols..41
  Vulnerabilities and Risks 42
  Best Practices for Users 44

Chapter 10: The Role of Validators in the Solana Network......46
  Understanding Validators..46
  How Validators Operate 47
  Importance of Validators in Decentralization...................49

Chapter 11: Solana's Ecosystem: Key Projects and Partnerships 50
  Major Projects Built on Solana 50
  Strategic Partnerships..52
  Community Contributions..54

Chapter 12: Future Trends in Solana: Predictions and Insights 56
  Potential Developments..56
  Market Trends..57
  The Future of Solana in the Crypto Space 59

Chapter 1: Introduction to Solana

Overview of Blockchain Technology

Blockchain technology is a decentralized digital ledger system that records transactions across many computers in such a way that the registered transactions cannot be altered retroactively. This technology ensures transparency, security, and efficiency in various applications, ranging from cryptocurrencies to supply chain management. Each transaction is grouped into blocks, which are then linked together in chronological order, forming a chain. This structure not only provides a clear audit trail but also eliminates the need for intermediaries, allowing peer-to-peer interactions.

One of the most important aspects of blockchain technology is its consensus mechanisms, which are protocols that consider a transaction valid and add it to the blockchain. Various consensus algorithms exist, each with its strengths and weaknesses. For instance, Proof of Work, used by Bitcoin, requires significant computational power, while Proof of Stake, employed by many newer blockchains, including Solana, is less resource-intensive and encourages users to hold and stake their tokens to validate transactions. Solana's unique approach, known as Proof of History, timestamps transactions to improve efficiency and throughput, enabling it to process thousands of transactions per second.

Blockchain technology also facilitates the creation of decentralized applications (dApps) that operate on a blockchain network. Developers can build these applications using smart contracts, which are self-executing contracts with the terms of the agreement directly written into code. This capability not only enhances automation but also reduces the risk of fraud and manipulation. Solana provides an array of tools and resources for developers, making it an attractive platform for building dApps that can cater to various sectors, including finance, gaming, and social networks.

The rise of decentralized finance (DeFi) has been one of the most significant developments within the blockchain space. DeFi platforms utilize blockchain technology to recreate traditional financial systems, such as lending, borrowing, and trading, but in a decentralized manner. Solana has emerged as a formidable player in this arena, offering lower transaction fees and quicker processing times compared to its competitors like Ethereum. This has led to a surge in DeFi projects on the Solana blockchain, fostering innovation and expanding financial access to a broader audience.

As blockchain technology continues to evolve, so do the challenges and opportunities within its ecosystem. Security remains a primary concern, as vulnerabilities can lead to significant losses. Solana has implemented various security features, including a robust validator network that protects against attacks. Additionally, the growth of NFT marketplaces on Solana has opened new avenues for creators and investors alike, presenting both opportunities and challenges. Understanding these dynamics is crucial for anyone looking to navigate the blockchain landscape effectively, especially as future trends and innovations continue to shape this rapidly changing field.

The Emergence of Solana

Solana was founded in 2017 by Anatoly Yakovenko, who aimed to create a high-performance blockchain capable of processing thousands of transactions per second. The project emerged from a need for a scalable solution in the cryptocurrency space, particularly as existing blockchains struggled with congestion and high fees during peak usage times. Unlike many other blockchain platforms, Solana was designed from the ground up to prioritize speed and efficiency, making it an attractive option for developers and users alike. The introduction of its unique consensus mechanism, Proof of History, played a pivotal role in distinguishing Solana from its competitors.

Proof of History allows for the validation of transactions without requiring every participant in the network to reach consensus on the order of events. This innovative approach reduces the time taken to confirm transactions, enabling Solana to achieve unprecedented throughput. By leveraging cryptographic timestamps, the network can sequence events efficiently, which is particularly beneficial for applications requiring rapid interactions, such as decentralized finance (DeFi) platforms and non-fungible token (NFT) marketplaces. This focus on speed and efficiency has contributed to Solana's rapid growth and adoption within the blockchain ecosystem.

The developer community has also played a significant role in Solana's emergence. With a rich set of tools and resources, developers are encouraged to build on the platform, contributing to a vibrant ecosystem of decentralized applications (dApps). Solana's user-friendly programming environment, which supports popular languages like Rust and C, lowers the barrier to entry for developers. This flexibility allows for a diverse range of projects, from DeFi innovations to NFT platforms, further solidifying Solana's position in the competitive blockchain landscape.

As Solana gained traction, it began to attract significant investments and partnerships, which have been critical to its growth. Major venture capital firms recognized the potential of Solana's technology, leading to substantial funding rounds that have fueled development and marketing efforts. Furthermore, strategic collaborations with existing blockchain projects and platforms have expanded Solana's reach and utility, allowing it to integrate with various ecosystems and attract users from different sectors.

Looking ahead, Solana's emergence marks a significant shift in the blockchain landscape. With its commitment to scalability, speed, and developer accessibility, the platform is well-positioned to continue its upward trajectory. As the cryptocurrency market evolves and the demand for efficient solutions grows, Solana's innovations will likely play a crucial role in shaping the future of decentralized applications and services. The ongoing developments within the Solana ecosystem will be essential to monitor, as they hold the potential to redefine how users and developers interact with blockchain technology.

Chapter 2: Understanding the SOL Blockchain

Key Features of Solana

Solana's architecture is designed to provide high throughput and low latency, making it a standout in the blockchain landscape. One of the most significant features is its ability to process transactions at an impressive speed, with claims of up to 65,000 transactions per second under optimal conditions. This high throughput is achieved through a combination of innovations, including its unique consensus mechanism known as Proof of History, which timestamps transactions to create a historical record that proves the order and passage of time between events. This not only facilitates faster transactions but also enhances the overall efficiency of the network.

Another key feature of Solana is its scalability. Unlike many other blockchains that struggle to maintain performance as they grow, Solana employs a series of techniques, such as parallel transaction processing, which allows it to handle multiple transactions simultaneously. This is in stark contrast to traditional blockchains that process transactions sequentially. By utilizing a technology called Sealevel, Solana can execute smart contracts in parallel, which significantly reduces bottlenecks and enhances the capacity of the network to scale with demand.

Security is also a fundamental aspect of Solana's design. The network utilizes a robust mechanism that combines elements of both Proof of Stake and Proof of History, ensuring that validators are incentivized to uphold the integrity of the network. Validators play a crucial role in maintaining security by confirming transactions and creating new blocks. This dual-layer approach not only secures the network against malicious attacks but also ensures that the transaction history remains immutable, which is vital for maintaining trust in decentralized applications built on the platform.

In addition to its technical features, Solana boasts a vibrant ecosystem that supports various applications, particularly in the realms of decentralized finance (DeFi) and non-fungible tokens (NFTs). The platform has attracted numerous projects that leverage its capabilities, offering innovative solutions for asset trading, lending, and more. NFT marketplaces on Solana have seen substantial growth, presenting unique opportunities for creators and collectors alike. This burgeoning ecosystem is further strengthened by partnerships and collaborations with significant players in the crypto space, enhancing the platform's visibility and adoption.

Lastly, the community and developer support surrounding Solana are essential features that contribute to its success. With a growing number of resources, tools, and documentation available for developers, building on Solana has become increasingly accessible. This supportive environment fosters innovation and encourages the development of new projects that leverage the blockchain's capabilities. As the demand for scalable and efficient blockchain solutions continues to rise, Solana is well-positioned to play a pivotal role in shaping the future of decentralized technologies.

Use Cases for Solana

Solana has emerged as a prominent player in the blockchain space, offering a diverse range of use cases that cater to various sectors. One of the most significant use cases is decentralized finance (DeFi). Solana's high throughput and low transaction costs enable developers to create robust DeFi applications that can handle thousands of transactions per second. This scalability allows for innovative financial products such as decentralized exchanges, lending platforms, and liquidity pools, which are gaining traction among users looking for efficient alternatives to traditional finance. The rapid growth of DeFi on Solana showcases its potential to disrupt existing financial systems and offer more inclusive financial services.

Another critical use case for Solana lies in the realm of non-fungible tokens (NFTs). The platform's speed and low fees make it an attractive environment for creating and trading NFTs. Artists and creators can mint their digital assets without incurring prohibitive costs, while buyers enjoy a seamless purchasing experience. Solana has seen a surge in NFT marketplaces, which facilitate the buying, selling, and trading of unique digital items. This has opened up new opportunities for creators to monetize their work and for collectors to invest in digital assets, thereby expanding the NFT ecosystem significantly.

Gaming is also a burgeoning use case on the Solana blockchain. The ability to process high volumes of transactions quickly is essential for blockchain-based games, where user interactions can occur in real-time. Solana supports the development of play-to-earn games, where players can earn cryptocurrency rewards for their in-game activities. These innovative gaming models not only enhance user engagement but also create economic opportunities for players, contributing to the growing intersection of gaming and blockchain technology.

In addition to DeFi, NFTs, and gaming, Solana's infrastructure is well-suited for enterprise applications. The blockchain's security features, scalability, and performance make it an ideal choice for businesses looking to leverage blockchain technology for various use cases, such as supply chain management, data integrity, and identity verification. Companies can build decentralized applications (dApps) on Solana to improve transparency and efficiency in their operations, gaining a competitive edge in their respective industries.

Lastly, the Solana blockchain is increasingly being utilized for social impact initiatives. Projects aimed at promoting financial inclusion, environmental sustainability, and community empowerment are finding a home on Solana. The low transaction costs and fast confirmation times enable organizations to implement solutions that reach underserved populations. This trend highlights the versatility of the Solana network, demonstrating its capacity to support not only profitable ventures but also initiatives that aim to create a positive social impact.

Chapter 3: Solana's Consensus Mechanism: Exploring Proof of History

What is Proof of History?

Proof of History (PoH) is a unique cryptographic technique utilized by the Solana blockchain to enhance its consensus mechanism. Unlike traditional blockchains that rely on timestamps from nodes to establish the order of transactions, PoH creates a historical record that proves that an event has occurred at a specific moment in time. This mechanism allows validators in the Solana network to efficiently agree on the order of transactions without the need for extensive communication and synchronization, significantly improving the network's throughput and speed.

The essence of PoH lies in its ability to generate a verifiable delay function, which creates a sequence of hashes that are time-stamped. Each hash is linked to a previous one, forming a chain that serves as a reliable ledger of events. This process not only records the passage of time but also assures that the data has not been altered since it was recorded. By providing a clear and immutable history of transactions, PoH facilitates faster processing times and reduces the computational load on the network. This is particularly important for applications that require high throughput, such as decentralized finance (DeFi) and non-fungible tokens (NFTs).

In the context of Solana, PoH works in tandem with a proof-of-stake (PoS) consensus mechanism. While PoH establishes the order of transactions, PoS allows validators to confirm those transactions based on their stake in the network. This dual approach enhances security and efficiency, enabling Solana to process thousands of transactions per second. As a result, the network can accommodate a growing number of users and applications without compromising performance, making it an attractive option for developers and investors alike.

The implementation of PoH also addresses common challenges faced by other blockchain networks, such as scalability and latency. By streamlining the process of reaching consensus, Solana can maintain low transaction costs while ensuring rapid processing times. This is a significant advantage over competitors like Ethereum, where congestion can lead to high fees and slower transaction speeds. The ability to handle large volumes of transactions efficiently opens up new opportunities for innovation within the Solana ecosystem.

In summary, Proof of History is a foundational element of the Solana blockchain that enhances its overall functionality and performance. By creating a reliable and verifiable time-stamped history of transactions, PoH allows for improved scalability, efficiency, and security. As the blockchain landscape continues to evolve, understanding PoH will be crucial for anyone looking to invest in or develop on the Solana platform. Its unique approach positions Solana as a leader in the space, paving the way for new trends and advancements in decentralized applications and finance.

How Proof of History Works

Proof of History (PoH) is a unique cryptographic technique that plays a pivotal role in the Solana blockchain's consensus mechanism. Unlike traditional consensus algorithms that rely on various forms of time-stamping or block confirmation, PoH creates a historical record that proves that an event has occurred at a specific moment in time. This function is not merely a timestamp but a verifiable way to establish the sequence of events, thereby enhancing the efficiency and speed of the blockchain. By generating a continuous and cryptographically secure sequence of hashes, PoH allows validators to confirm the order of transactions without needing to communicate extensively with each other.

The implementation of PoH significantly reduces the time required to reach consensus on transaction ordering. In a typical blockchain, nodes must exchange messages to ensure they all agree on the state of the ledger, which can lead to delays and a bottleneck effect. With PoH, the need for extensive messages is minimized since the historical record itself serves as proof. This record allows validators to quickly and accurately verify the order of transactions, leading to faster block times and increased throughput. Consequently, Solana can process thousands of transactions per second, making it one of the fastest blockchains available.

Moreover, the process of generating Proof of History makes use of a verifiable delay function (VDF). This function ensures that even though the result can be quickly verified, it takes a predetermined amount of time to compute. This characteristic is critical because it prevents malicious actors from manipulating the time-stamping process, thereby maintaining the integrity of the blockchain. The VDF contributes to the overall security and reliability of the Solana network, as any attempt to alter the historical record would require an immense amount of computational power.

Another essential aspect of PoH is its compatibility with Solana's overall architecture. The integration of PoH with the Proof of Stake (PoS) consensus mechanism allows for a hybrid approach that enhances both scalability and security. Validators are incentivized to act honestly, as their stake in the network is directly tied to their performance. The combination of PoH and PoS not only streamlines the validation process but also contributes to a more decentralized and resilient network, as validators are spread across various geographic locations and are independent entities.

In summary, Proof of History is a groundbreaking innovation that positions Solana as a leader in the blockchain space. By establishing a reliable and efficient method for time-stamping events, PoH addresses some of the most pressing challenges faced by traditional blockchains, such as scalability and speed. As more developers and investors explore the possibilities within the Solana ecosystem, understanding PoH will be crucial for appreciating how this technology sets Solana apart from its competitors and fosters a vibrant environment for decentralized applications and finance.

Benefits of Proof of History

Proof of History (PoH) is a groundbreaking innovation that enhances the efficiency and functionality of the Solana blockchain. By providing a verifiable and time-stamped record of events, PoH allows nodes within the network to agree on the chronological order of transactions without needing to communicate extensively with one another. This capability significantly reduces the time and resources typically required for consensus in traditional blockchains, leading to faster transaction speeds and lower latency. For individuals learning about crypto and potential investors, understanding PoH is crucial as it underpins Solana's ability to handle high throughput and scale effectively.

One of the primary benefits of Proof of History is its contribution to scalability. Solana's architecture can process thousands of transactions per second, a feat that traditional blockchains often struggle to achieve. By embedding timestamps directly into the blockchain, PoH eliminates the need for complex consensus algorithms that can slow down transaction processing. This feature makes Solana particularly appealing for developers looking to build decentralized applications (dApps) and for investors interested in projects that require high performance and responsiveness to user demands.

Another significant advantage of PoH is its role in enhancing security. The time-stamped nature of PoH creates an immutable record of transactions that is resistant to manipulation. Since each entry in the blockchain is linked to a specific moment in time, any attempt to alter the history of transactions would require an immense amount of computational effort, making fraud or double-spending extremely difficult. For those exploring the security aspects of blockchain technology, PoH represents a robust mechanism that can help instill confidence in the integrity of the Solana network.

In terms of developer experience, Proof of History streamlines the process of building on Solana. By providing a reliable and consistent framework for timekeeping, developers can focus on creating innovative features rather than grappling with the complexities of transaction verification and order. This ease of development not only accelerates the pace of innovation on the platform but also attracts a diverse range of projects, from DeFi applications to NFT marketplaces. For investors, this vibrant ecosystem offers numerous opportunities to engage with cutting-edge technologies and emerging trends.

Lastly, Proof of History positions Solana favorably in the competitive landscape of blockchain technology. With its unique approach to consensus, Solana differentiates itself from established platforms like Ethereum, which rely on proof-of-work or proof-of-stake mechanisms. The ability to maintain high throughput while ensuring security and reliability makes Solana an attractive option for both developers and investors. As the blockchain space continues to evolve, PoH could play a pivotal role in shaping the future of decentralized systems, making it essential for those interested in crypto to grasp its significance in the broader context of blockchain innovation.

Chapter 4: Developing on Solana: Tools and Resources for Developers

Programming Languages Supported

Solana is designed to accommodate a variety of programming languages, which enhances its accessibility for developers coming from different backgrounds. The primary language used for developing smart contracts on the Solana blockchain is Rust. Rust offers a high level of performance and safety, making it an ideal choice for developers who prioritize efficiency and reliability in their applications. The language's strict compiler checks help prevent common programming errors, resulting in more secure and robust code. Developers familiar with systems programming will find Rust particularly advantageous when building on Solana.

In addition to Rust, Solana also supports the C programming language. C is one of the most widely used programming languages in the world, known for its performance and low-level memory manipulation capabilities. This support for C allows developers who have experience in traditional software development to transition smoothly to blockchain programming. The ability to leverage existing knowledge in C can accelerate the development process, making it easier for developers to create complex decentralized applications (dApps) on the Solana platform.

Another language gaining traction within the Solana ecosystem is Solidity, primarily known for its use in Ethereum smart contracts. While Solidity is not natively supported on Solana, developers can use various tools to facilitate the migration of smart contracts from Ethereum to Solana. This interoperability is crucial for attracting developers who are already invested in the Ethereum ecosystem, allowing them to explore the unique advantages that Solana offers, such as higher throughput and lower transaction costs.

The flexibility of language support in Solana also extends to JavaScript, particularly for front-end development. Many decentralized applications require a user interface, and JavaScript is a dominant language for web development. Solana provides a rich set of libraries and tools that enable developers to build interactive user interfaces that communicate seamlessly with Solana's backend. This integration allows for a more cohesive development experience, bridging the gap between smart contracts and user-facing applications.

Overall, the variety of programming languages supported by Solana enhances its appeal to a broader range of developers. With options like Rust, C, and JavaScript, Solana provides a versatile environment that caters to both seasoned blockchain developers and those new to the field. This flexibility is instrumental in fostering innovation within the Solana ecosystem, encouraging the growth of diverse applications that leverage the unique capabilities of the SOL blockchain. As the ecosystem continues to evolve, the support for multiple programming languages will likely play a pivotal role in attracting new talent and driving the development of cutting-edge decentralized solutions.

Development Frameworks and Libraries

In the rapidly evolving landscape of blockchain technology, development frameworks and libraries play a critical role in simplifying the process of building decentralized applications (dApps). On the Solana blockchain, developers have access to a rich ecosystem of tools designed to facilitate the creation of high-performance applications. These frameworks and libraries streamline the development process, allowing both seasoned developers and newcomers to engage with the Solana network efficiently. By leveraging these resources, developers can focus on building innovative features rather than grappling with the underlying complexities of the blockchain.

One of the most popular frameworks for Solana development is Anchor, which provides a robust foundation for building secure and scalable smart contracts. Anchor simplifies the programming model by introducing a set of conventions and abstractions that reduce boilerplate code and enhance developer productivity. Furthermore, it integrates seamlessly with Rust, the primary programming language used for Solana smart contracts, ensuring that developers can write, test, and deploy their applications with ease. The framework also includes built-in support for common tasks such as managing accounts and handling errors, which can significantly reduce development time and increase the reliability of applications.

In addition to Anchor, developers can utilize a variety of other libraries and tools that enhance the functionality of dApps on Solana. For instance, the Solana Web3.js library enables JavaScript developers to interact with the Solana blockchain directly from web applications. This library provides a simple and intuitive API for sending transactions, querying account balances, and more, making it an essential tool for front-end developers looking to build user-friendly interfaces for their dApps. Moreover, the availability of various SDKs allows for the integration of Solana with popular frameworks like React and Vue, further broadening the accessibility of Solana development.

Tooling for testing and deployment is also crucial for ensuring that applications are robust and secure. The Solana CLI (Command Line Interface) is an essential tool that enables developers to manage their projects, deploy smart contracts, and interact with the Solana network. Coupled with testing libraries like Mocha or Chai, developers can write comprehensive tests to validate their code before deploying it to the mainnet. This emphasis on testing promotes a culture of quality and security within the Solana development community, which is vital given the increasing focus on security in the blockchain space.

As the Solana ecosystem continues to grow, the importance of these development frameworks and libraries will only increase. By providing developers with the tools they need to create innovative applications efficiently, Solana is positioning itself as a leading platform for decentralized finance (DeFi), non-fungible tokens (NFTs), and other blockchain-based solutions. As more developers adopt these frameworks and libraries, the potential for groundbreaking applications on Solana expands, paving the way for new trends and innovations that can transform the cryptocurrency landscape.

Resources for Learning and Support

In the rapidly evolving world of blockchain technology, having access to the right resources can significantly enhance your understanding of the Solana blockchain and its myriad functionalities. For beginners and investors alike, numerous online platforms offer comprehensive courses, tutorials, and articles that delve into the intricacies of Solana. Websites such as Solana's official documentation provide a solid foundation, covering everything from basic concepts to advanced technical details. These resources are essential for grasping the unique aspects of Solana, including its consensus mechanism, Proof of History, and how it differentiates itself from other blockchains like Ethereum.

For those interested in developing on Solana, a wealth of tools and resources is available to facilitate learning and project creation. The Solana Developer Portal offers extensive documentation, code examples, and SDKs that empower developers to build decentralized applications (dApps) efficiently. Community-driven resources, such as forums and Discord channels, also play a crucial role in providing support and fostering collaboration among developers. Engaging with these platforms not only helps in troubleshooting but also allows developers to share insights and innovations, thereby enhancing the broader Solana ecosystem.

Investors looking to navigate the decentralized finance (DeFi) landscape on Solana can benefit from a variety of analytical tools and market research platforms. Websites such as DeFi Llama and CoinGecko provide real-time data on DeFi projects, token performance, and liquidity metrics specific to Solana. Understanding these resources is vital for making informed investment decisions. Additionally, participating in community initiatives and webinars can offer insights into emerging trends and innovations within the DeFi space on Solana, enabling investors to capitalize on opportunities as they arise.

The NFT marketplace on Solana has gained significant traction, and various resources cater to individuals looking to explore this niche further. Platforms like Magic Eden and Solanart provide not only marketplaces for purchasing and selling NFTs but also educational content about the intricacies of NFT creation and trading. Learning about the challenges and opportunities within this vibrant space is essential for both creators and collectors, and these dedicated resources serve as a launchpad for understanding market dynamics and community engagement.

Finally, keeping abreast of the latest developments in Solana's ecosystem is crucial for anyone involved with the blockchain. Following industry news sources, subscribing to newsletters, and engaging with social media channels dedicated to Solana can help individuals stay informed about key projects, partnerships, and future trends. Resources such as the Solana Foundation's blog and community updates are invaluable for understanding the ongoing evolution of the network. By leveraging these diverse resources, individuals can enhance their knowledge and participation in the Solana blockchain, ultimately leading to a more informed and engaged community.

Chapter 5: Solana vs. Ethereum: A Comparative Analysis

Performance Metrics

Performance metrics play a crucial role in understanding the efficiency and effectiveness of the Solana blockchain. These metrics provide insights into various aspects of the network's operation, such as transaction speed, throughput, and overall reliability. For investors and developers alike, grasping these metrics is essential for assessing the health and viability of the Solana ecosystem. By measuring performance, stakeholders can better evaluate their strategies, whether in trading, developing applications, or participating in decentralized finance initiatives.

One of the most notable performance metrics for Solana is its transaction speed. The network boasts an impressive capability to process thousands of transactions per second (TPS), significantly surpassing many of its competitors, including Ethereum. This high throughput is largely attributed to Solana's unique consensus mechanism, Proof of History, which allows for efficient verification of transactions. Understanding this metric is vital for anyone looking to engage with the network, as it directly impacts user experience and the feasibility of scalable applications built on Solana.

Another key performance metric is latency, which refers to the time it takes for a transaction to be confirmed. Solana has made strides in minimizing latency, achieving confirmation times of around 400 milliseconds on average. This low latency is especially important for applications that require real-time interactions, such as gaming and high-frequency trading platforms. Investors and developers must consider this metric when analyzing the potential of Solana-based applications, as a high-performance network can lead to greater user adoption and satisfaction.

Throughput is another essential metric that indicates the total number of transactions processed within a given time frame. Solana's architecture allows it to achieve a throughput exceeding 65,000 TPS under optimal conditions. This capability supports a wide range of decentralized applications, from finance to non-fungible tokens (NFTs), making Solana an attractive option for developers. By comparing Solana's throughput with that of other blockchains, stakeholders can gauge its competitive advantage in the rapidly evolving crypto landscape.

Finally, understanding the economic implications of performance metrics is crucial for investors. High performance in terms of speed and throughput often translates into increased user engagement and, consequently, higher demand for SOL tokens. As the ecosystem grows and more projects are developed on the Solana blockchain, the interaction between performance metrics and market dynamics will become increasingly relevant. Investors should keep these correlations in mind when making decisions, as performance metrics can serve as indicators of potential growth and long-term sustainability within the Solana network.

Ecosystem and Community

The Solana ecosystem is a vibrant and rapidly expanding network that brings together developers, investors, and users in the world of decentralized applications and blockchain technology. At the heart of this ecosystem lies a diverse range of projects that leverage Solana's unique features, such as its high throughput and low transaction costs. This thriving environment is not only conducive to innovation but also fosters collaboration among various stakeholders who are eager to contribute to the platform's growth. Understanding the components of this ecosystem is essential for anyone looking to navigate the Solana landscape effectively.

One of the key aspects of the Solana ecosystem is its focus on scalability and performance. The blockchain is designed to handle thousands of transactions per second, making it a suitable platform for projects that require fast and efficient processing. This scalability draws numerous developers who create decentralized applications (dApps) across various sectors, including finance, gaming, and non-fungible tokens (NFTs). The presence of such a wide array of projects enhances the overall utility of the network, attracting both users and investors who are eager to participate in this burgeoning space.

Community plays a crucial role in the success of the Solana network. The Solana community consists of enthusiastic developers, dedicated validators, and engaged users who collectively contribute to the platform's development and governance. Community-driven initiatives, such as hackathons and educational workshops, help to nurture talent and encourage new projects to emerge. This collaborative spirit not only strengthens the network but also creates a sense of belonging among participants, which is essential for long-term sustainability in the competitive blockchain space.

In addition to its supportive community, Solana boasts a rich ecosystem of partnerships and integrations that enhance its capabilities. Collaborations with established companies and projects in the crypto space provide Solana with the resources and expertise needed to expand its reach and functionality. These partnerships often lead to innovative solutions that address pressing challenges within the blockchain industry, such as interoperability and user experience. As the ecosystem continues to evolve, the synergy between Solana and its partners will be instrumental in driving further adoption and growth.

As interest in blockchain technology and decentralized finance continues to rise, the Solana ecosystem is well-positioned to capitalize on these trends. With its commitment to scalability, community engagement, and strategic partnerships, Solana is not only attracting attention from investors but also paving the way for future innovations. By understanding the dynamics of the Solana ecosystem, participants can better navigate the opportunities and challenges that lie ahead, making informed decisions that align with their goals in the crypto space.

Use Cases and Adoption

Use cases and adoption of the Solana blockchain have rapidly evolved, showcasing its versatility across various sectors. The architecture of Solana enables high throughput and low transaction costs, making it an attractive platform for developers and businesses alike. One prominent use case is in decentralized finance (DeFi), where Solana hosts numerous protocols that offer lending, borrowing, and trading services. Projects such as Serum and Raydium exemplify how Solana's capabilities allow for seamless financial transactions, setting the stage for innovative financial products and services without the bottlenecks often seen on other blockchains.

In addition to DeFi, the non-fungible token (NFT) marketplace has seen considerable growth on the Solana network. Artists and creators are leveraging Solana's fast and low-cost transactions to mint and sell NFTs, providing an alternative to Ethereum's often prohibitive fees. Platforms like Metaplex have emerged to facilitate NFT creation and distribution, enabling artists to reach audiences without the traditional barriers. This explosive growth in the NFT sector not only enhances Solana's appeal but also attracts a diverse range of users and investors looking to capitalize on the burgeoning digital art market.

Solana's scalability solutions also play a significant role in its adoption. The unique Proof of History consensus mechanism allows the network to process thousands of transactions per second, significantly more than Ethereum and many other blockchains. This scalability is critical for applications requiring high transaction volumes, such as gaming and real-time data applications. Projects like Star Atlas illustrate how this capability can support complex, interactive gaming experiences that depend on instant transactions, thus broadening Solana's use cases beyond finance and art.

Moreover, the Solana ecosystem is bolstered by strategic partnerships and collaborations. The involvement of major players in the crypto space, including integrations with well-known wallets and exchanges, has heightened the visibility and reliability of the Solana network. These collaborations not only foster growth but also attract developers who are keen to build on a platform that promises both innovation and stability. As more projects choose to build within Solana's ecosystem, the network's utility and adoption continue to expand.

Looking ahead, the future trends in Solana's adoption appear promising. As the demand for decentralized applications (dApps) rises, Solana is well-positioned to capitalize on this trend due to its technical advantages. Additionally, ongoing developments in security features and user experience enhancements will likely draw even more users and investors to the platform. With a robust community and a forward-thinking approach, Solana is set to become a significant player in the blockchain landscape, driving further adoption and use case diversification.

Chapter 6: Decentralized Finance (DeFi) on Solana: Trends and Innovations

Overview of DeFi on Solana

Decentralized Finance (DeFi) on Solana is a rapidly evolving sector that leverages the unique capabilities of the Solana blockchain to provide financial services without intermediaries. By offering high throughput and low transaction costs, Solana has positioned itself as an attractive platform for DeFi projects seeking to capitalize on the growing demand for decentralized applications. This overview examines the core attributes that make Solana a compelling choice for DeFi developers and users, highlighting the innovations and trends shaping this vibrant ecosystem.

At the heart of Solana's appeal is its impressive scalability, which allows for thousands of transactions per second. This capability is enabled by its unique consensus mechanism, Proof of History, which streamlines the process of transaction validation and significantly reduces the time needed for confirmations. As a result, DeFi applications on Solana can execute complex financial transactions quickly and efficiently, catering to the needs of users who require speed and reliability. This efficiency not only enhances user experience but also enables developers to create more sophisticated financial products that can attract a wider audience.

The DeFi landscape on Solana has seen a surge of innovative projects, ranging from decentralized exchanges (DEXs) to lending platforms and yield farming protocols. These projects leverage Solana's infrastructure to offer features such as automated market making, liquidity pools, and cross-chain capabilities. The low fees associated with transactions on Solana further encourage participation, making it feasible for users to engage in micro-transactions that may not be economically viable on other blockchains. This has led to a diverse array of financial services becoming accessible to a broader audience, including those who may have previously been excluded from traditional finance.

In addition to the existing projects, the DeFi space on Solana is characterized by a continuous influx of new entrants and innovations. Developers are actively exploring new models for liquidity provision, governance mechanisms, and automated trading strategies. As the community grows, so does the competition, prompting projects to differentiate themselves through unique features and user incentives. This dynamic environment fosters creativity and experimentation, which are crucial for the long-term sustainability and growth of the DeFi sector on Solana.

As DeFi continues to expand on the Solana blockchain, it is essential for both investors and users to stay informed about the trends and developments within this ecosystem. The integration of new technologies, partnerships, and regulatory considerations will shape the future of DeFi on Solana. By understanding the current landscape and the potential for future innovations, participants can better navigate the opportunities and challenges that lie ahead in this exciting domain of decentralized finance.

Major DeFi Projects

The decentralized finance (DeFi) landscape on the Solana blockchain has rapidly evolved, presenting significant opportunities for investors and developers alike. Major DeFi projects on Solana have emerged as key players in the ecosystem, leveraging the platform's high throughput and low transaction costs to deliver innovative financial services. Among these, projects like Serum, Raydium, and Mango Markets stand out, each contributing unique functionalities that cater to various aspects of the DeFi space.

Serum is a decentralized exchange (DEX) that is built specifically for Solana, designed to provide a fast and efficient trading experience. It utilizes an order book model, which distinguishes it from many other DEXs that operate on automated market-making principles. This allows Serum to offer advanced trading features such as limit orders and cross-chain trading capabilities. By integrating with Solana's architecture, Serum achieves impressive performance metrics, enabling users to execute trades with minimal latency and lower fees, which is crucial for high-frequency trading strategies.

Raydium is another prominent player in the Solana DeFi ecosystem, functioning as an automated market maker (AMM) and liquidity provider. It not only offers users the ability to swap tokens but also facilitates liquidity farming, where users can earn rewards by providing liquidity to various trading pairs. Raydium's unique feature is its integration with Serum's order book, allowing liquidity providers to access deeper liquidity and improved pricing. This synergy between Raydium and Serum exemplifies the collaborative nature of DeFi on Solana, fostering a robust environment for users and developers.

Mango Markets rounds out the trio of major DeFi projects on Solana, focusing on decentralized margin trading and lending. It offers users the ability to trade with leverage, which can amplify potential returns but also increases risk exposure. Mango Markets utilizes Solana's fast transaction speeds to enable real-time price updates and efficient margin calls, making it an attractive option for traders looking to capitalize on market movements. The platform's emphasis on user experience and security has garnered it a loyal user base, further solidifying its position within the DeFi space.

These major DeFi projects on Solana not only illustrate the platform's capabilities but also highlight the growing trend of innovation within the ecosystem. As developers continue to build on Solana, the landscape is likely to expand, introducing new financial products and services that cater to the evolving needs of users. For investors and newcomers to the crypto space, understanding these projects is essential, as they represent some of the most promising opportunities within the burgeoning DeFi sector on the Solana blockchain.

Future of DeFi on Solana

The future of Decentralized Finance (DeFi) on the Solana blockchain is poised for significant growth and innovation, thanks to its unique architecture and capabilities. Solana's Proof of History consensus mechanism facilitates fast transaction speeds and scalability, making it an attractive platform for DeFi applications. As the demand for decentralized financial services continues to rise, Solana's infrastructure can support a myriad of projects, potentially outpacing competitors like Ethereum in terms of efficiency and cost-effectiveness.

One of the key trends in Solana's DeFi landscape is the increasing integration of cross-chain functionalities. As users seek to leverage assets across multiple blockchain networks, projects on Solana are developing innovative solutions that enable interoperability. This trend not only enhances liquidity but also broadens the accessibility of DeFi applications, allowing users to transfer assets seamlessly between Solana and other blockchains. Such integrations could lead to a more interconnected financial ecosystem, fostering greater user engagement and investment opportunities.

Moreover, the rise of automated market makers (AMMs) and lending platforms on Solana reflects a robust trend towards creating user-friendly interfaces and experiences. As developers continue to build on Solana, they are focusing on simplifying the user experience for both novice and experienced investors. This emphasis on usability, combined with the network's low transaction fees, is likely to attract a larger audience to DeFi on Solana. Enhanced user experiences will play a crucial role in onboarding new users and driving adoption in the coming years.

Security remains a top priority for DeFi projects, and Solana's architecture offers features that can enhance the safety of decentralized applications. As the ecosystem evolves, developers are increasingly focused on building security measures that protect users' assets and data. With the growth of decentralized insurance protocols and auditing services, users can expect an elevated level of security when interacting with DeFi applications on Solana. This focus on security will be essential in building trust and confidence within the community, ensuring the longevity of DeFi initiatives on the platform.

Looking ahead, the potential for DeFi on Solana is immense, bolstered by strategic partnerships and community support. As the Solana ecosystem expands, collaborations with traditional finance and fintech companies could further legitimize and enhance the DeFi offerings on the chain. The continuous innovation from developers, along with a dedicated community, positions Solana as a formidable player in the DeFi space. With ongoing advancements and a growing user base, the future of DeFi on Solana promises to be marked by transformative developments that could redefine the landscape of decentralized finance.

Chapter 7: NFT Marketplaces on Solana: Opportunities and Challenges

Overview of NFTs on Solana

Non-fungible tokens (NFTs) have gained significant attention in the digital landscape, and the Solana blockchain has emerged as a prominent platform for their creation and trade. NFTs on Solana leverage the network's high throughput and low transaction costs, making it an attractive option for artists, creators, and collectors. Unlike traditional cryptocurrencies, NFTs represent unique digital assets, which can include anything from artwork to virtual real estate. Solana's capabilities enable these assets to be minted and transferred efficiently, fostering a vibrant ecosystem for both creators and investors.

The architecture of Solana plays a crucial role in supporting the NFT market. Solana's consensus mechanism, known as Proof of History (PoH), allows for rapid transaction confirmations and enhances scalability. This is particularly beneficial for NFT projects that require fast interactions, such as auctions or real-time trading. The ability to process thousands of transactions per second means that users can engage with NFTs without the delays often seen on other blockchains, such as Ethereum. As a result, the user experience on Solana is smoother, encouraging more participants to enter the NFT space.

Several NFT marketplaces have emerged on the Solana blockchain, each offering unique features and opportunities. Platforms like Solanart and DigitalEyes enable creators to showcase their work and collectors to discover new pieces. These marketplaces benefit from Solana's low fees, which allow for microtransactions that would be impractical on other networks. As a result, even smaller artists can participate in the NFT market without incurring prohibitive costs. The diversity of marketplaces also fosters competition, driving innovation and improving the overall user experience.

The NFT landscape on Solana is not without its challenges. As the market continues to grow, issues such as copyright infringement and the need for more robust verification systems have emerged. Furthermore, the influx of projects can lead to market saturation, making it difficult for new artists to gain visibility. To address these challenges, the Solana community is actively working on developing standards and best practices that promote transparency and security. This collaborative effort is essential for maintaining trust within the ecosystem and ensuring the long-term viability of NFTs on Solana.

Looking ahead, the future of NFTs on Solana appears promising. With ongoing developments in technology and infrastructure, the platform is poised to attract even more creators and investors. The expansion of decentralized finance (DeFi) solutions also opens new avenues for NFT utilization, such as collateralized loans and fractional ownership. As the ecosystem evolves, it will be crucial for participants to stay informed about trends and innovations, positioning themselves to capitalize on the ever-changing landscape of NFTs within the Solana blockchain.

Key NFT Marketplaces

The emergence of non-fungible tokens (NFTs) has transformed the digital asset landscape, and Solana's blockchain has quickly become a prominent platform for NFT transactions. Several key marketplaces have emerged within the Solana ecosystem, providing users with diverse options for buying, selling, and trading NFTs. These platforms leverage Solana's high throughput and low transaction fees, making them attractive for both creators and collectors. Understanding these marketplaces is essential for anyone interested in exploring the world of NFTs on Solana.

Magic Eden stands out as one of the largest and most popular NFT marketplaces on Solana. Launched in 2021, it has quickly gained traction due to its user-friendly interface and extensive collection of NFTs ranging from artwork to virtual real estate. The platform offers features such as a launchpad for new projects, allowing creators to mint and list their NFTs easily. Additionally, Magic Eden has introduced various tools for users to track their collections and engage with the community, making it a go-to destination for both novice and experienced NFT enthusiasts.

Another noteworthy marketplace is Solanart, which was one of the first NFT platforms on Solana. Solanart has established itself as a reliable venue for discovering and purchasing unique digital art. The platform emphasizes the authenticity of NFTs, allowing creators to showcase their work while ensuring buyers can purchase verified pieces. With a focus on art and collectibles, Solanart has cultivated a niche audience, appealing to those specifically interested in artistic NFTs and unique digital assets.

DigitalEyes is also gaining popularity within the Solana NFT ecosystem. This marketplace aims to provide a seamless experience for users by offering a range of features, including a simple listing process for creators and a robust search function for buyers. DigitalEyes focuses on community engagement, with initiatives to promote emerging artists and projects. Its commitment to supporting the Solana NFT community sets it apart, making it an attractive option for those looking to explore new and innovative digital art.

Finally, the Solsea marketplace is noteworthy for its integration of metadata and royalties for NFT creators. By allowing creators to embed licenses and other information directly into their NFTs, Solsea provides a unique advantage that appeals to artists and developers alike. This feature enhances the value proposition for creators, enabling them to ensure that their work is appropriately credited and compensated. As the NFT landscape continues to evolve, Solsea's focus on creator rights positions it as a meaningful player in the Solana NFT marketplace arena.

Challenges Facing NFT Adoption

The rapid growth of non-fungible tokens (NFTs) has garnered significant attention within the crypto space, yet several challenges hinder their widespread adoption. One of the primary obstacles is the issue of scalability. As NFT transactions often require substantial computational power and storage, networks can become congested, leading to slow transaction times and increased fees. For users and creators looking to mint, buy, or sell NFTs, these issues can result in a frustrating experience, ultimately deterring participation in the NFT market. Solana, with its high throughput capabilities, offers a solution, but the interoperability with other networks remains a concern for many users.

Another significant challenge lies in the educational barrier surrounding NFTs. Many potential users and investors lack a clear understanding of what NFTs are and how they function within the broader blockchain ecosystem. This gap in knowledge can lead to skepticism and reluctance to engage with NFTs, especially among traditional investors unfamiliar with digital assets. Education initiatives from both the Solana community and NFT marketplaces are crucial to demystifying the technology and illustrating its value. Without effective communication of the benefits and uses of NFTs, widespread acceptance will continue to lag.

Moreover, the environmental impact of NFTs has become a pressing issue. Concerns about the carbon footprint associated with blockchain transactions, especially on networks that rely on energy-intensive proof-of-work mechanisms, have sparked debates. While Solana utilizes a proof-of-history consensus mechanism that significantly reduces energy consumption, the broader narrative surrounding NFTs still grapples with environmental sustainability. Addressing these concerns through transparent practices and showcasing eco-friendly solutions will be essential for fostering trust and promoting adoption among environmentally conscious users.

Legal and regulatory uncertainties also pose challenges for NFT adoption. The lack of clear guidelines regarding ownership rights, copyright issues, and the classification of NFTs can create confusion and apprehension among creators and investors. As governments and regulatory bodies begin to examine the crypto space more closely, the evolving legal landscape may impact how NFTs are created, bought, and sold. Stakeholders in the Solana ecosystem must remain vigilant and proactive in advocating for clear regulations that protect users while fostering innovation.

Finally, the market's speculative nature can deter long-term investment in NFTs. Many current participants are driven by the potential for quick profits rather than a genuine interest in the art or assets themselves. This speculative behavior can lead to volatility and price manipulation, which ultimately undermines the perceived value of NFTs. For sustained adoption, the focus should shift towards building a more robust community that values creativity, utility, and long-term engagement with NFTs. Encouraging responsible investment practices and highlighting projects with genuine artistic or functional merit will be vital in establishing a more stable and trustworthy NFT market.

Chapter 8: Scalability Solutions in Solana: What Sets It Apart

Architecture of Solana

The architecture of Solana is designed to facilitate high throughput and low latency, making it a formidable contender in the blockchain landscape. At its core, Solana employs a unique combination of technologies and methodologies that distinguish it from other blockchains. By integrating the Proof of History consensus mechanism with a robust architecture, Solana is able to process thousands of transactions per second while maintaining security and decentralization. This design allows developers to build applications that can scale effectively, catering to a growing user base without compromising on performance.

Central to Solana's architecture is its innovative approach to consensus. The Proof of History mechanism serves as a cryptographic clock that enables nodes to agree on the order of events in the network. This is in contrast to traditional consensus algorithms that require extensive communication among nodes to validate transactions. By timestamping transactions, Solana reduces the overhead typically associated with maintaining consensus, thus improving overall network efficiency. This design choice not only enhances transaction speeds but also supports the creation of decentralized applications that require quick and reliable interactions.

In addition to its consensus mechanism, Solana's architecture incorporates an optimized data structure known as the Sealevel runtime. Sealevel allows for parallel transaction processing, enabling the network to handle multiple transactions simultaneously rather than sequentially. This capability significantly boosts throughput and ensures that applications can scale seamlessly as demand increases. Developers leveraging this feature can build more complex and interactive decentralized applications (dApps) that are capable of serving a vast number of users without experiencing slowdowns.

Another critical aspect of Solana's architectural design is its innovative use of smart contracts, known as programs in the Solana ecosystem. These programs are designed to run efficiently within the network's runtime environment, utilizing the capabilities of Solana's architecture to execute transactions with minimal latency. The Solana development ecosystem offers a variety of tools and resources that empower developers to create robust dApps, enhance user experiences, and explore the potential of decentralized finance (DeFi) and non-fungible tokens (NFTs) within the Solana framework.

Finally, Solana's architecture is complemented by a vibrant ecosystem of validators, projects, and partnerships that contribute to its reliability and security. Validators play a crucial role in maintaining the network's integrity, ensuring that transactions are processed accurately and efficiently. As the Solana ecosystem continues to grow, its architectural foundations provide the necessary support for innovative projects and applications, paving the way for future trends and developments in the blockchain space. This robust architecture not only positions Solana as a leader in scalability and performance but also invites ongoing exploration and investment in its burgeoning ecosystem.

Innovations in Scalability

Innovations in scalability are crucial for the continued growth and adaptation of blockchain technologies, particularly in the context of the Solana blockchain. As the demand for decentralized applications (dApps) and services increases, the ability to efficiently process a high volume of transactions becomes paramount. Solana's unique approach to scalability combines several innovative strategies, allowing it to handle thousands of transactions per second without sacrificing security or decentralization. This capability positions Solana as a leading platform in the competitive blockchain landscape.

One of the key innovations in Solana's scalability is its use of the Proof of History (PoH) consensus mechanism. PoH establishes a verifiable order of events in a way that is efficient and secure, enabling the network to process transactions in parallel rather than sequentially. This parallelization significantly reduces the time it takes to confirm transactions, allowing the network to maintain high throughput even during peak usage periods. By integrating PoH with a robust Proof of Stake (PoS) mechanism, Solana ensures that the network remains both fast and secure, addressing one of the common challenges faced by blockchain platforms.

Moreover, Solana's architecture employs a unique transaction processing model that distinguishes it from traditional blockchains. Instead of relying on a single chain of blocks, Solana utilizes a series of parallelizable transaction processing units, which allows for the simultaneous execution of multiple transactions. This design minimizes bottlenecks and enhances the overall efficiency of the network. By adopting this innovative strategy, Solana can support a wide range of applications, from high-frequency trading in decentralized finance (DeFi) to the minting and trading of non-fungible tokens (NFTs).

In addition to its core technological innovations, Solana also emphasizes developer accessibility through a variety of tools and resources. The availability of robust software development kits (SDKs) and comprehensive documentation makes it easier for developers to build scalable applications on the Solana platform. This focus on developer experience not only accelerates the creation of new dApps but also fosters a vibrant ecosystem where innovation thrives. As more developers create solutions tailored to the needs of users, the overall scalability of the network improves, creating a positive feedback loop.

Finally, the future of scalability in Solana looks promising, as the platform continues to evolve and adapt to the needs of its users. Ongoing research and development efforts aim to further enhance transaction speeds and reduce latency, ensuring that Solana remains competitive in the rapidly changing blockchain environment. As the ecosystem expands, the innovations in scalability will play a pivotal role in attracting new projects and users, solidifying Solana's position as a leading blockchain for decentralized applications and services.

Comparison with Other Blockchains

When comparing Solana to other blockchains, Ethereum often emerges as a key point of reference due to its established presence and extensive developer community. Ethereum utilizes a Proof of Work consensus mechanism, which has been transitioning to Proof of Stake to enhance scalability and reduce energy consumption. In contrast, Solana employs a unique Proof of History (PoH) combined with Proof of Stake, enabling it to process transactions at an unprecedented speed of up to 65,000 transactions per second. This significant difference in architecture allows Solana to effectively tackle issues related to congestion and high fees that have historically plagued Ethereum, particularly during peak usage periods.

Another blockchain that often comes up in discussions about scalability is Binance Smart Chain (BSC). BSC has gained popularity for its low transaction fees and fast confirmation times. However, it operates on a more centralized model compared to Solana, which relies on a diverse network of validators. This decentralization is a cornerstone of Solana's design, fostering greater security and resistance to censorship.

While BSC's architecture can facilitate rapid transactions, Solana's innovative approach to consensus and transaction validation positions it as a more robust option for applications requiring both speed and security.

Cardano is another notable blockchain that presents a contrast to Solana. Cardano emphasizes academic research and a slow, methodical approach to development, focusing on building a secure and sustainable ecosystem. However, this caution often results in slower implementation of features compared to Solana's rapid development cycle. Solana's focus on real-world applicability and its commitment to providing developers with comprehensive tools and resources has led to a vibrant ecosystem, especially in areas like decentralized finance (DeFi) and non-fungible tokens (NFTs). The speed and efficiency of Solana's network make it an appealing choice for developers looking to launch innovative projects quickly.

When examining the NFT landscape, Solana stands out against competitors like Ethereum and Flow. While Ethereum remains the leading platform for NFTs, high gas fees can deter artists and collectors. Solana addresses this concern with significantly lower transaction costs and faster processing times, enabling a more fluid marketplace for creators and buyers alike. Moreover, the rapid growth of NFT marketplaces on Solana showcases its potential to redefine how digital assets are created and traded, fostering a new wave of innovation that leverages its unique features.

Finally, looking at the future trends within the blockchain space, Solana's approach to scalability and performance presents a compelling case for its continued growth and adoption. As more developers and projects flock to its ecosystem, Solana is well-positioned to compete with and even surpass other blockchains in various niches, particularly in DeFi and NFT markets. Its unique consensus mechanism, coupled with a commitment to decentralization and security, places Solana at the forefront of blockchain technology, challenging other platforms to innovate and adapt in response.

Chapter 9: Security Features of the Solana Blockchain

Security Protocols

Security protocols are a fundamental aspect of any blockchain network, including Solana, which has gained attention for its innovative approach to scalability and efficiency. In the context of the SOL blockchain, security protocols are designed to protect the integrity of transactions, safeguard user data, and ensure that the network remains resilient against various forms of attacks. By understanding these protocols, investors and developers can better appreciate the measures in place that help maintain the trustworthiness of the Solana ecosystem.

One of the key components of Solana's security framework is its unique consensus mechanism, Proof of History (PoH). This mechanism allows the network to create a historical record that proves that an event has occurred at a specific moment in time. PoH works in tandem with the more traditional Proof of Stake (PoS) model, which helps to validate transactions and secure the network. By integrating time into the consensus process, Solana can achieve high throughput and low latency while maintaining a secure environment for its users.

In addition to the consensus mechanisms, Solana employs several cryptographic techniques to enhance security. These include hashing algorithms that secure transaction data and public-private key cryptography that enables users to maintain control over their assets. The combination of these cryptographic principles ensures that transactions are not only verifiable but also resistant to tampering. This is crucial for both personal security and the broader integrity of the network, especially as decentralized finance (DeFi) applications and non-fungible tokens (NFTs) continue to grow in popularity on the platform.

Another significant aspect of Solana's security protocols involves its validator network. Validators are responsible for processing transactions and maintaining the network's overall health. Solana has implemented a rigorous selection process for validators, which includes incentives for good behavior and penalties for malicious actions. This structure encourages a decentralized network of trustworthy participants, reducing the risk of centralization and the potential for collusion or fraud. As new projects and partnerships emerge within the Solana ecosystem, the role of validators becomes increasingly vital in ensuring that these developments are secure and reliable.

Overall, the security protocols within the Solana blockchain are designed to create a robust and trustworthy environment for users and developers alike. By leveraging advanced technologies and innovative consensus mechanisms, Solana not only addresses common security concerns but also positions itself as a competitive player in the evolving landscape of blockchain technology. As more individuals and organizations engage with the SOL blockchain, understanding these security protocols will be essential for navigating the opportunities and challenges that lie ahead in the world of cryptocurrency and decentralized applications.

Vulnerabilities and Risks

Vulnerabilities and risks are inherent in any blockchain ecosystem, including Solana, despite its innovative design and rapid growth. One primary concern is the potential for smart contract vulnerabilities. As developers create decentralized applications (dApps) on the Solana blockchain, they must ensure their code is secure and free of exploits. Bugs or flaws in smart contracts can lead to significant financial losses and undermine user trust. The complexity of programming languages used in blockchain development, such as Rust and C, can introduce additional challenges, making it crucial for developers to prioritize rigorous testing and auditing.

Another critical risk associated with the Solana network is its reliance on a network of validators. While these validators play a vital role in maintaining the integrity and security of the blockchain through the Proof of History consensus mechanism, their decentralization is a concern. If a significant number of validators are compromised or act maliciously, it could lead to network disruptions or even attacks. Additionally, the performance of the network can be impacted if a subset of validators fails to keep up with transaction demands, which could affect the overall user experience and confidence in the platform.

Scalability, a hallmark feature of Solana, presents its own set of vulnerabilities. Although the blockchain can process thousands of transactions per second, this high throughput could lead to potential security trade-offs. During peak usage, the network may experience congestion, which can expose the system to denial-of-service attacks. Moreover, as more projects build on the Solana blockchain, the increasing demand on its infrastructure might strain its capabilities, necessitating ongoing enhancements to maintain performance and security.

The landscape of decentralized finance (DeFi) and non-fungible tokens (NFTs) on Solana is rapidly evolving, but it is not without risks. Users engaging with DeFi protocols may encounter issues related to liquidity, impermanent loss, and the inherent volatility of crypto assets. Additionally, the proliferation of NFT marketplaces can lead to challenges such as counterfeit assets and the potential for scams. Users should exercise caution and conduct thorough research before investing in these emerging sectors to mitigate their exposure to fraud and misinformation.

Lastly, the regulatory environment surrounding cryptocurrencies and blockchain technology continues to evolve, posing another layer of risk for Solana and its users. As governments around the world seek to establish frameworks for digital assets, changes in regulations could impact the functionality and accessibility of the Solana ecosystem. Investors and developers must stay informed about regulatory developments to navigate this uncertain landscape effectively. Understanding these vulnerabilities and risks is essential for anyone engaging with the Solana blockchain to make informed decisions and safeguard their investments.

Best Practices for Users

When engaging with the Solana blockchain, users should prioritize security as a fundamental best practice. This includes using hardware wallets or reputable software wallets that offer robust security features. Ensuring that private keys are stored securely and never shared is essential to protect assets from unauthorized access. Additionally, users should enable two-factor authentication whenever possible, providing an extra layer of security against potential threats. Keeping software and wallet applications updated is crucial, as updates often include important security patches that safeguard against vulnerabilities.

Another best practice is to conduct thorough research before investing in any projects or tokens within the Solana ecosystem. The rapid growth of decentralized finance (DeFi) and non-fungible tokens (NFTs) on Solana has led to numerous opportunities, but it also presents risks, particularly with new and unverified projects. Users should analyze project whitepapers, assess the credibility of development teams, and follow community discussions on platforms like Discord and Twitter. Engaging with established resources and educational content will help users make informed decisions and avoid potential scams.

Understanding and participating in the governance of the Solana network can also enhance the user experience. Solana is a decentralized blockchain, and many projects within its ecosystem involve community governance. Users should familiarize themselves with governance tokens, voting mechanisms, and the implications of their participation in decision-making processes. By engaging in governance, users can influence the direction of projects they believe in and contribute to the overall health and decentralization of the network.

Users should also remain aware of the evolving landscape of Solana's ecosystem, including its scalability solutions and innovations. Solana's unique consensus mechanism, Proof of History, significantly enhances transaction speed and throughput, making it an attractive option for developers and investors alike. Staying updated on network upgrades, new partnerships, and technological advancements will help users capitalize on emerging trends and opportunities. Following reputable news sources and joining community forums can provide insights into these developments.

Lastly, participating actively in the Solana community can enrich the user experience and provide valuable networking opportunities. Engaging with other users, developers, and investors through social media, forums, and events fosters a sense of belonging and can lead to collaborative opportunities. By sharing knowledge and experiences, users contribute to the collective growth of the Solana ecosystem while gaining insights that can inform their investment strategies and development efforts.

Chapter 10: The Role of Validators in the Solana Network

Understanding Validators

Validators play a crucial role in the Solana blockchain, serving as the backbone of its consensus mechanism. In the context of Solana, a validator is a node that participates in the process of validating transactions and producing new blocks. Unlike traditional proof-of-work systems, where miners compete to solve complex mathematical puzzles, Solana employs a unique consensus mechanism called Proof of History (PoH). This innovation allows validators to timestamp transactions efficiently, creating a verifiable order of events that enhances the overall speed and efficiency of the network.

To become a validator on the Solana network, an individual or organization must meet certain requirements, including having a robust hardware setup and a reliable internet connection. The minimum specifications often include powerful CPUs, sufficient RAM, and SSD storage to handle the high transaction throughput Solana is known for. Additionally, potential validators must stake a certain amount of SOL tokens, which serves as a security deposit. This staking mechanism not only aligns the incentives of validators with the health of the network but also provides a deterrent against malicious behavior, as any wrongdoing can lead to slashing of their staked tokens.

The responsibilities of validators extend beyond merely confirming transactions. They are also tasked with maintaining the overall security and integrity of the blockchain. This involves monitoring the network for any signs of attacks, ensuring their nodes are always operational, and participating in governance decisions that affect the network's future. Validators play a vital role in Solana's decentralized ecosystem, contributing to its resilience and stability, which is critical for attracting developers and users to the platform.

In return for their services, validators earn rewards in the form of newly minted SOL tokens and transaction fees. The distribution of these rewards is designed to incentivize a healthy and competitive environment among validators. As more participants join the network, the stakes increase, leading to more robust security and better performance. This dynamic creates an ecosystem where both established validators and newcomers can thrive, provided they adhere to the network's standards and maintain operational excellence.

Understanding the role of validators is essential for anyone looking to invest in or develop on the Solana blockchain. As the ecosystem grows, the demand for reliable validators will only increase. Investors should consider the performance and reputation of validators when staking their tokens, while developers can leverage the insights about validator operations to optimize their applications. The interplay between validators and the broader Solana network is a fundamental aspect of its design, directly influencing its scalability and efficiency, making it a critical topic in the exploration of Solana's unique offerings.

How Validators Operate

Validators play a crucial role in the Solana blockchain, ensuring the network operates smoothly and securely. Each validator is responsible for processing transactions, maintaining the integrity of the blockchain, and participating in the consensus mechanism. In Solana, this mechanism is unique due to its incorporation of Proof of History (PoH), which allows validators to timestamp transactions and create a verifiable order of events. This innovation significantly enhances the efficiency of the network, enabling it to handle thousands of transactions per second.

To become a validator on the Solana network, an individual or organization must first set up the necessary infrastructure. This involves acquiring powerful hardware, including high-performance servers, and ensuring a stable internet connection. The validator must also install the Solana software and synchronize with the blockchain. Once operational, the validator will begin to receive and validate transactions, contributing to the network's security and performance. This process requires a deep understanding of the technology and a commitment to maintaining high uptime and reliability.

Validators are incentivized to perform their duties effectively through a system of rewards. Each time a validator successfully processes a transaction and adds it to the blockchain, they earn SOL tokens as compensation. This reward system not only motivates validators to maintain high performance but also aligns their interests with the overall health of the network. However, if a validator behaves maliciously or fails to perform adequately, they can face penalties, including the potential loss of staked tokens. This mechanism reinforces the importance of trustworthy participation in the network.

The delegation process allows SOL token holders to support validators without having to run a node themselves. Token holders can delegate their tokens to a chosen validator, thereby contributing to the validator's stake. In return, they receive a portion of the rewards generated by that validator. This system fosters a decentralized approach, as it enables a wider range of participants to engage with the network while ensuring that validators have the necessary resources to operate effectively.

Overall, the operation of validators is fundamental to the functionality of the Solana blockchain. Their role in processing transactions, securing the network, and participating in the consensus mechanism ensures that Solana can maintain its high throughput and low latency. As the ecosystem continues to grow, understanding the intricacies of validator operations will be essential for anyone looking to navigate the world of Solana, whether as an investor, developer, or enthusiast.

Importance of Validators in Decentralization

Validators play a crucial role in the decentralization of the Solana blockchain, acting as the backbone of the network's security and operational efficiency. In the context of blockchain technology, validators are responsible for verifying transactions, maintaining the integrity of the ledger, and ensuring that the network operates smoothly without central authority. Their involvement is essential for the decentralized nature of the blockchain, as it allows for a distributed approach to governance and consensus, minimizing the risk of control by a single entity.

The Solana network employs a unique consensus mechanism known as Proof of History (PoH), which enhances the efficiency of validators in processing transactions. This innovative approach allows validators to generate timestamps for transactions, creating a verifiable chronology that significantly reduces the time needed to reach consensus. By leveraging PoH, validators can confirm transactions at high speed, which is a significant advantage for applications requiring rapid processing, such as decentralized finance (DeFi) platforms and NFT marketplaces. This efficiency not only improves user experience but also attracts developers and businesses looking to build on a scalable blockchain.

Moreover, the decentralization facilitated by validators fosters a more secure network. With numerous validators operating independently, the risk of a single point of failure is significantly reduced. Attackers would need to compromise a majority of validators to manipulate the network, which is a daunting task given the distribution of nodes. This decentralized security model encourages trust among users and investors, as it minimizes vulnerabilities that can arise from centralized systems. As more validators join the network, the overall resilience and security of the Solana ecosystem increase, making it an attractive option for those looking to invest in cryptocurrencies.

Validators also play a key role in governance within the Solana ecosystem. They participate in decision-making processes that shape the future of the network, including protocol upgrades and changes to transaction fees. This participatory model ensures that the interests of a diverse group of stakeholders are represented, rather than being dictated by a central authority. As the Solana community grows, the engagement of validators becomes increasingly important, as their voices help steer the development of the blockchain in a direction that benefits all users.

Finally, the importance of validators extends beyond technical functionality; they are integral to the overall health and growth of the Solana ecosystem. The presence of active validators encourages more users to engage with the network, leading to increased transaction volume and investment opportunities. As the ecosystem expands, the demand for validators will also rise, creating a virtuous cycle that enhances decentralization. Understanding the role of validators is essential for anyone interested in the Solana blockchain, as they are pivotal in ensuring that the network remains robust, secure, and decentralized.

Chapter 11: Solana's Ecosystem: Key Projects and Partnerships

Major Projects Built on Solana

Major projects built on the Solana blockchain showcase the platform's versatility and capacity to support a range of applications from decentralized finance (DeFi) to non-fungible tokens (NFTs). One of the most notable projects is Serum, a decentralized exchange that leverages Solana's high throughput and low latency to offer a seamless trading experience. Serum aims to provide a fully decentralized ecosystem with a central limit order book, differentiating itself from other decentralized exchanges that often rely on automated market makers. This design allows for greater liquidity and better price discovery, making it an attractive option for traders and liquidity providers alike.

Another prominent project within the Solana ecosystem is Raydium, an automated market maker that integrates with Serum. Raydium enables users to trade assets quickly and efficiently while also providing yield farming opportunities. Its unique feature is the ability to leverage Serum's order book, which allows users to access deeper liquidity and execute trades at optimal prices. This combination of AMM and order book functionalities positions Raydium as a key player in the DeFi landscape on Solana, demonstrating the potential for innovative financial products built on this blockchain.

In the realm of NFTs, Metaplex stands out as a significant initiative that enhances the creation and management of non-fungible tokens on Solana. Metaplex provides a suite of tools that simplify the process for creators to mint, sell, and manage their NFT collections. With built-in storefront functionality, Metaplex empowers artists and developers to launch their NFT projects without requiring extensive technical knowledge. This democratization of NFT creation is critical in fostering a vibrant digital art and collectibles market, further solidifying Solana's position in the NFT space.

The gaming sector has also embraced Solana, with projects like Star Atlas leading the charge. Star Atlas is a grand strategy game that incorporates blockchain technology to create a play-to-earn ecosystem where players can earn real-world value through in-game activities. The integration of NFTs allows for true ownership of in-game assets, creating a new paradigm for gamers. Star Atlas exemplifies how Solana's high transaction speeds and low fees make it an ideal platform for developing complex and engaging gaming experiences that can attract a broad audience.

Lastly, the rise of decentralized identity solutions, such as Solana's Civic integration, illustrates the blockchain's potential beyond just finance and entertainment. Civic provides a secure and efficient way for users to manage their digital identities, enhancing privacy and reducing the risk of identity theft. By leveraging Solana's robust infrastructure, Civic aims to create a more secure internet experience, showcasing the diverse applications that can be built on the SOL blockchain. These major projects collectively highlight Solana's capabilities and its growing ecosystem, making it a compelling option for investors and developers alike.

Strategic Partnerships

Strategic partnerships play a crucial role in the growth and development of the Solana blockchain ecosystem. These collaborations enhance the platform's capabilities, expand its reach, and drive innovation across various sectors. By aligning with other projects, companies, and organizations, Solana fosters an environment that supports developers, investors, and users alike. This not only strengthens the network but also facilitates the adoption of decentralized applications, DeFi solutions, and NFTs, which are pivotal to Solana's vision.

One of the significant advantages of strategic partnerships is the pooling of resources and expertise. For example, partnerships with leading technology firms can provide developers with access to advanced tools and infrastructure, thereby accelerating the development of applications on the Solana network. By integrating with established platforms, Solana can tap into existing user bases and leverage shared technologies, enhancing the overall functionality and appeal of its blockchain. This collaborative approach is essential for creating a robust ecosystem that can compete effectively with other blockchains, such as Ethereum.

Moreover, partnerships in the DeFi space are particularly impactful. Solana has formed alliances with various DeFi projects that aim to provide innovative financial solutions, such as lending, borrowing, and yield farming. These collaborations not only enrich the offerings available on the Solana network but also attract a wider audience of investors and users interested in decentralized finance. As these partnerships continue to evolve, they help position Solana as a leading player in the rapidly growing DeFi sector, fostering greater liquidity and user engagement.

The NFT marketplace is another area where strategic partnerships have proven beneficial. Collaborations with artists, creators, and established NFT platforms enable Solana to cultivate a vibrant ecosystem for digital assets. By providing a user-friendly environment for minting, buying, and selling NFTs, these partnerships enhance the platform's visibility and appeal. As the NFT space continues to expand, Solana's strategic alliances can drive innovation, ensuring that artists and collectors alike have access to the tools and resources necessary for success.

Looking ahead, the importance of strategic partnerships in the Solana ecosystem cannot be overstated. As the blockchain landscape continues to evolve, the ability to adapt and collaborate with other innovative projects will be critical for maintaining a competitive edge. By fostering a culture of partnership and cooperation, Solana is well-positioned to capitalize on future trends and insights, driving further growth and adoption of its blockchain technology. This collaborative spirit will not only benefit individual projects but also contribute to the overall health and sustainability of the Solana ecosystem.

Community Contributions

Community contributions play a vital role in the growth and sustenance of the Solana blockchain ecosystem. As a decentralized platform, Solana thrives on the active participation of its community members, encompassing developers, investors, artists, and enthusiasts. This collective effort not only fosters innovation but also creates a vibrant environment where ideas can flourish. The community's engagement is evident in various forms, from building decentralized applications (dApps) to organizing events that promote education and awareness about the Solana blockchain.

One of the most significant ways the community contributes is through the development of dApps and tools that enhance the functionality of the Solana network. Developers leverage the unique features of Solana, such as its high throughput and low transaction costs, to create solutions that cater to diverse needs. These contributions range from DeFi protocols that offer users new financial opportunities to NFT marketplaces that enable artists to showcase and sell digital art. The collaborative nature of the community ensures that these projects are continuously iterated upon, resulting in a dynamic ecosystem that attracts users and investors alike.

Education and advocacy are also crucial components of community contributions. Many community members dedicate their time to providing resources, tutorials, and workshops aimed at demystifying the Solana blockchain for newcomers. This educational outreach is essential for empowering investors and developers, as it equips them with the knowledge needed to navigate the complexities of blockchain technology. By fostering a culture of learning, the community helps to lower barriers to entry, encouraging more individuals to participate in the Solana ecosystem.

Moreover, events and hackathons organized by the community serve as platforms for networking and collaboration. These gatherings not only bring together developers and investors but also facilitate discussions about the future of the Solana blockchain. Participants share insights, showcase their projects, and form partnerships that can lead to innovative solutions. Such events are instrumental in building a sense of camaraderie and shared purpose among community members, reinforcing the idea that the success of Solana is a collective endeavor.

In conclusion, the contributions of the Solana community are integral to the platform's ongoing evolution. From developing cutting-edge applications to promoting education and fostering collaboration, community members play a pivotal role in shaping the future of the Solana blockchain. As more individuals engage with the ecosystem, the potential for innovation and growth continues to expand, positioning Solana as a leading player in the ever-evolving landscape of decentralized technologies.

Chapter 12: Future Trends in Solana: Predictions and Insights

Potential Developments

As the Solana blockchain continues to evolve, several potential developments are on the horizon that could significantly impact its ecosystem. One of the most noteworthy areas of advancement is the ongoing enhancement of scalability solutions. While Solana is already recognized for its high throughput and low transaction fees, further innovations in layer-2 solutions and sharding could improve network efficiency. These advancements aim to accommodate increasing user demand and support more complex DeFi applications and NFT marketplaces, positioning Solana as a leading platform in the competitive blockchain landscape.

Another promising area for potential development lies in the integration of advanced security features. As the blockchain space matures, so does the need for robust security protocols. Initiatives aimed at improving the security of smart contracts and transaction verification processes are likely to emerge. This focus on security will not only protect users' assets but also enhance trust in the Solana network among investors and developers. Solutions such as formal verification tools and enhanced auditing processes may become standard practices, fostering a more secure environment for all participants within the ecosystem.

The role of validators in the Solana network is also expected to evolve. As the network grows, so will the complexity of the validator responsibilities. Innovations aimed at increasing validator decentralization and incentivizing more participants could lead to a more resilient network. This could involve implementing new governance models or reward structures that encourage active participation. A thriving community of validators will not only secure the network but also contribute to its decision-making processes, ultimately shaping the future trajectory of the Solana ecosystem.

Additionally, the competitive landscape of blockchain technology will drive Solana to differentiate itself further from its rivals, particularly Ethereum. As Ethereum continues to transition toward Ethereum 2.0, Solana's unique features, such as its Proof of History consensus mechanism, will play a critical role in attracting developers and projects. Potential collaborations or integrations with other emerging technologies, such as artificial intelligence and the Internet of Things, could further enhance Solana's appeal. This adaptability will be crucial as the blockchain space matures and user expectations evolve.

Lastly, the decentralized finance (DeFi) sector is poised for significant growth within the Solana ecosystem. As new projects emerge and existing ones expand, the demand for innovative financial products and services will likely increase. This trend may lead to the development of cross-chain solutions that allow for greater interoperability with other blockchain platforms. Furthermore, as more users engage with DeFi on Solana, educational resources and tools will become essential to help newcomers navigate this complex landscape. Overall, the future of Solana is filled with potential developments that could redefine its impact on the blockchain industry.

Market Trends

The market trends surrounding the Solana blockchain reflect a rapidly evolving landscape that resonates with the growing interest in decentralized technologies. As one of the leading platforms in the realm of cryptocurrency, Solana has captured attention due to its unique consensus mechanism, Proof of History, which enhances transaction speeds and scalability.

Investors and developers alike are keenly observing these trends as they indicate the platform's potential to address current limitations seen in other blockchains, particularly Ethereum. This shift towards efficient consensus mechanisms is reshaping investor confidence and driving increased adoption among developers looking for a robust blockchain solution.

Decentralized Finance (DeFi) has emerged as a significant trend within the Solana ecosystem, showcasing innovations that appeal to both users and investors. With lower transaction fees and faster processing times compared to its competitors, Solana has become a preferred choice for DeFi applications. The rise of decentralized exchanges, lending protocols, and yield farming platforms on Solana signifies a growing appetite for these financial tools. Investors are navigating this landscape with keen interest, as the potential for high returns is coupled with the risks inherent to emerging technologies. Understanding these DeFi trends is crucial for those looking to capitalize on the opportunities within the Solana blockchain.

The NFT marketplace on Solana is another trend garnering attention, as it presents both opportunities and challenges. With the explosion of digital art and collectibles, Solana's low fees and high throughput attract creators and collectors. While the platform's rapid growth offers ample opportunities for innovation, it also faces challenges such as market saturation and the need for robust security measures. Investors are closely monitoring these developments, as successful projects within the NFT space could lead to significant returns. The interplay between market demand and the platform's capabilities will be crucial in shaping the future of NFTs on Solana.

Scalability remains a defining characteristic of Solana, setting it apart from other blockchains and creating a favorable environment for growth. The network's ability to handle thousands of transactions per second without compromising security is a trend that investors find particularly appealing. As more projects launch on Solana, this scalability will be tested, and the platform's resilience will play a significant role in its long-term viability. By understanding the scalability solutions Solana offers, both developers and investors can better assess the platform's potential in a competitive market.

Lastly, the Solana ecosystem is enriched by key projects and partnerships that are indicative of its market trends. Collaborations with established companies and innovative startups are driving the expansion of Solana's reach and functionality. As these partnerships develop, they not only enhance the platform's offerings but also instill confidence in potential investors. Keeping an eye on these strategic alliances will provide valuable insights into the direction of Solana and its position in the ever-evolving blockchain space. Understanding the intricate dynamics of these market trends will empower individuals to make informed decisions in their crypto journey.

The Future of Solana in the Crypto Space

The future of Solana in the crypto space appears promising, driven by its innovative architecture and the growing adoption of decentralized applications (dApps). As a high-performance blockchain, Solana has garnered attention for its impressive scalability, enabling thousands of transactions per second without compromising security or decentralization. This capability positions Solana as a strong contender in the blockchain landscape, particularly as the demand for efficient and user-friendly platforms continues to rise. With its unique Proof of History consensus mechanism, Solana distinguishes itself from other blockchains, offering a compelling foundation for developers and investors alike.

One of the key factors influencing Solana's future is its expanding ecosystem, which includes a diverse range of projects and partnerships. Notable developments in decentralized finance (DeFi) and non-fungible tokens (NFTs) have created a vibrant marketplace that attracts users and developers. As more projects build on Solana, the network's utility and value proposition increase. This growth trend is likely to continue, as the platform provides the tools and resources necessary for developers to innovate and create compelling dApps. The increasing number of applications on Solana can drive user engagement, leading to a network effect that further enhances its position in the market.

Scalability remains a critical concern for blockchain networks, and Solana's approach to addressing this issue sets it apart from competitors, particularly Ethereum. Solana's architecture allows for parallel transaction processing, significantly improving throughput and reducing latency. This capability is essential for supporting high-demand applications, such as gaming and finance, which require rapid transaction speeds and low fees. As the user base expands and the demand for efficient transactions continues to grow, Solana's ability to maintain performance will be a crucial factor in its future success.

Security is another vital aspect of Solana's future trajectory. The network's design incorporates robust security features, including a decentralized validator network that enhances its resilience against attacks. As the crypto landscape evolves, maintaining high security standards will be imperative for building user trust and attracting institutional investment. Solana's focus on security, combined with its scalability and performance, positions it favorably in a market that is increasingly concerned with the vulnerabilities present in various blockchain solutions.

Looking ahead, the evolution of Solana will be shaped by ongoing innovations and the broader trends in the cryptocurrency space. As the market matures, Solana is likely to benefit from the increasing acceptance of blockchain technologies across various sectors. The rise of Web3 and the demand for decentralized solutions may further propel Solana's adoption, as users seek platforms that prioritize speed, security, and user experience. By continuing to foster a rich ecosystem of developers and projects, Solana is well-positioned to play a pivotal role in the future of decentralized applications and the overall evolution of the crypto landscape.

www.ingramcontent.com/pod-product-compliance
Lightning Source LLC
Chambersburg PA
CBHW062338220526
45469CB00008B/2756